Amazing Athletes ✧ Atletas increíbles

David Ortiz

Baseball Star ✧ Estrella del béisbol

Mary Ann Hoffman

Traducción al español: Eduardo Alamán

PowerKiDS press™ & **Editorial Buenas Letras**™
New York

Published in 2007 by The Rosen Publishing Group, Inc.
29 East 21st Street, New York, NY 10010

Book Design: Daniel Hosek
Layout Design: Lissette González

Photo Credits: Cover, p. 11 © Otto Greule Jr./Getty Images; p. 5 © Al Bello/Getty Images; p. 7 © Jamie Squire/Getty Images; p. 9 © Craig Melvin/Allsport; p. 13 © Donald Miralle/ Getty Images; pp. 15, 17 © Jed Jacobsohn/Getty Images; p. 19 © Jonathan Daniel/ Getty Images; p. 21 © Doug Pensinger/Getty Images.

Library of Congress Cataloging-in-Publication Data

Hoffman, Mary Ann, 1947-
  David Ortiz : baseball star / Mary Ann Hoffman.; traducción al español: Eduardo Alamán — 1st ed.
      p. cm. - (Amazing Athletes / Atletas increíbles)
  Includes index.
  ISBN-13: 978-1-4042-7599-7
  ISBN-10: 1-4042-7599-1
  1. Ortiz, David, 1975-—Juvenile literature. 2. Baseball players—Dominican Republic—Biography— Juvenile literature. 3. Spanish-language materials I. Title. II. Series.

Manufactured in the United States of America

Contents

Contenido

David Ortiz is a big man and a powerful hitter. He is called Big Papi.

David Ortiz es un hombre muy robusto y un bateador muy poderoso. Por eso le llaman Big Papi.

5

David was born in the Dominican Republic in 1975. He was signed by the Seattle Mariners in 1992.

David nació en 1975 en la República Dominicana. En 1992, fue contratado por los Marineros de Seattle.

David played for the Minnesota Twins from 1997 to 2002. He was hurt in 2001 and did not play many games.

David jugó para los Mellizos de Minnesota de 1997 al 2002. David no jugó muchos partidos en el 2001 porque estaba lastimado.

9

David joined the Boston Red Sox in 2003. He is a DH or designated hitter for the Red Sox.

David llegó a los Medias Rojas de Boston en 2003. David es el bateador designado de los Medias Rojas.

11

David is a left-handed hitter.
It is hard to strike him out.

David batea del lado izquierdo.
¡Es muy difícil ponchar a David!

David is known as a clutch hitter. A clutch hitter can hit the ball when it is most needed.

A David se le conoce como un bateador oportuno. Un bateador oportuno puede batear la pelota en los momentos más importantes.

15

The Boston Red Sox won the 2004 World Series. David hit the ball many times.

Los Medias Rojas de Boston ganaron la Serie Mundial en 2004. David bateó la pelota muchas veces.

17

David hit forty-seven home runs in 2005. He had never hit so many home runs in 1 year!

David bateó 47 jonrones en 2005. ¡David nunca había bateado tantos jonrones en un año!

19

David was named team MVP for the second year in a row in 2005. That means he was the most valuable player!

David fue elegido el Jugador más Valioso de su equipo en 2005. David recibió este honor dos años seguidos.

21

Glossary / Glosario

designated hitter (DEH-zihg-nay-tuhd HIH-tuhr) A player who bats in place of the pitcher.

home run (HOHM RUN) A hit in baseball that allows the batter to run around all four bases and score a run.

strike (STRYK) To swing at the ball and not hit it. To not swing at the ball when you should try to hit it.

World Series (WUHRLD SEER-eez) A number of games played every year to decide the best baseball team.

---

bateador designado (el) Jugador que batea en lugar del pitcher.

jonrón (el) Batazo que sale del campo y permite que el bateador recorra todas las bases para anotar una carrera.

ponchar Descalificar al bateador tras hacerlo abanicar tres veces al tratar de batear la pelota.

Serie Mundial (la) Partidos que se juegan cada año para determinar el mejor equipo.

Resources / Recursos

BOOKS IN ENGLISH / LIBROS EN INGLÉS

Gibbons, Gail. *My Baseball Book*. New York: Harper Collins Publishers, 2000.

Savage, Jeff. *David Ortiz*. Minneapolis, MN: Lerner Publishing Group, 2006.

BOOKS IN SPANISH / LIBROS EN ESPAÑOL

Suen, Anastasia. *La historia del béisbol*. New York: Rosen Publishing/Editorial Buenas Letras, 2004.

Index

Índice